CONTENTS

WWW.NONNAELDACOOKS.COM

THE FEAST OF THE 7 FISHES

It is traditional for Italian Catholics to abstain from eating red meat or poultry on the eve of a holiday, and instead eat fish and seafood. Christmas Eve, or "La Vigilia di Natale" is traditionally celebrated with a number of traditional dishes however they vary from region to region. The name "The Feast of the Seven Fishes" was actually created by Italians who came to North America and it has become popularized by American media in recent decades. Why seven fishes? Seven is a meaningful number for Catholics, there are seven sacraments, seven hills of Rome, etc. Also, we just like to be extra. Not just one, not just two, but at least seven different kinds of fish. Abbondanza!

Every town in Italy, and every family, has their own specific traditions that grow and change over time. Nonna Elda's family are Ciociara from the Frosinone region, so the dishes here will reflect those particular customs.

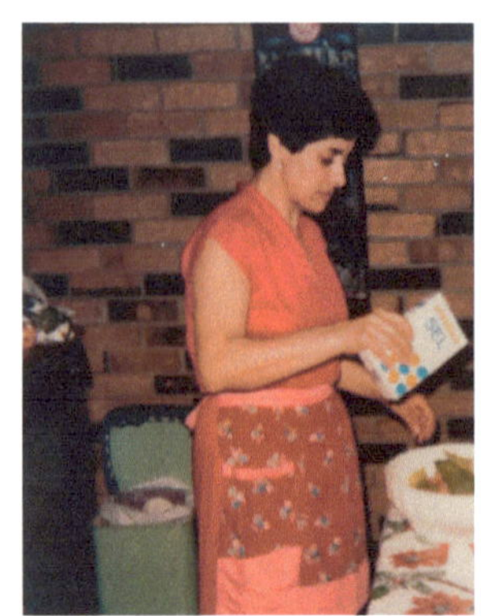

"MY GRANDMA LAURA USED TO SAY CHRISTMAS EVE YOU HAVE HAVE 35 DIFFERENT THINGS."
-ELDA

THOSE DIFFERENT THINGS DON'T NEED TO BE COMPLICATED DISHES, FOR EXAMPLE EACH KIND OF NUT, OR FRUIT, OR TYPE OF CHEESE COUNTS AS ONE THING.

ANTIPASTO

TIPS FOR CREATING AN AUTHENTIC AND DELICIOUS CHRISTMAS EVE ANTIPASTO SPREAD!

- Never cheap out on good cheese, Nonna loves pecorino, asiago, parmigiano reggiano.
- Try and get a variety of types of cheese made from different milks.
- Cantaloupe is often served with provolone cheese
- Olive mix, invest in good olives, Nonna always has five different kinds (each counts as one different thing towards the 35 flavours of Christmas)
- Add crackers, crostini,
- Focaccia (pg.6)
- Pickled vegetables such as eggplant (melanzane) or artichokes.
- Roasted Peppers (pg.5)
- Cold shrimp ring
- Calamari salad
- Insalata Baccalà (pg.7)
- Want to get fancy? Garnish with fresh herbs like rosemary sprigs

REMEMBER! NO MEAT!

WHY IS IT CALLED "ANTIPASTO"
IT SOUNDS LIKE YOU'RE PROTESTING AGAINST PASTA!

GOOD QUESTION!
THE NAME ANTIAPSTO IS
DERIVED FROM THE LATIN
LANGUAGE

"ANTI" MEANS "BEFORE"

"PASTUS" MEANS "MEAL"

SO "ANTIPASTO" LITERALLY
MEANS "BEFORE MEAL"

AS IT IS ALWAYS SERVED
BEFORE THE PASTA.

**TIP: CHEESE IS BEST SERVED
AT ROOM TEMPERATURE SO
REMEMBER TO TAKE YOUR
ANTIPASTO PLATTER OUT
ABOUT HALF AN HOUR
BEFORE YOUR GUESTS
ARRIVE.**

ROASTED PEPPERS

**SERVINGS: 5
PREP TIME: 10 MIN
REST TIME: 20 MINUTES
COOKING TIME:10-12 MINUTES**

INGREDIENTS

6 PEPPERS

EXTRA VIRGIN OLIVE OIL

SALT

HANDUL FRESH PARSLEY

1 TBSP OREGANO

6 CLOVES FRESH GARLIC

DIRECTIONS

- WASH BEFORE COOKING.
- BROIL 10-12 MIN OR BBQ
- REMOVE FROM OVEN AND PUT IN A POT AND COVER WITH LID UNTIL IT'S COOL, THIS WILL STEAM IT FOR EASY PEELING.
- CUT INTO LARGE SLICES
- SEASON AND SERVE AT ROOM TEMPERATURE

**THIS RECIPE KEEPS WELL IN THE FRIDGE FOR UP TO A WEEK, MAKE SURE THERE'S PLENTY OF OLIVE OIL.
IT'S ALSO EXCELLENT ON SANDWICHES!**

FOCACCIA PIZZA DOUGH

SERVINGS: 8
PREP TIME: 10 MIN
REST TIME: 2 HOURS
COOKING TIME: 30-35 MIN

INGREDIENTS
1 TSP YEAST
1 TBSP SUGAR
1 CUP WARM WATER
4 CUPS ALL PURPOSE FLOUR
(NONNA LOVES 5 ROSES FLOUR)
0.5 CUP WHOLE WHEAT FLOUR
3 TBSP OLIVE OIL
1 TSP SALT

DIRECTIONS
- MIX YEAST, SUGAR, AND WARM WATER IN A BOWL. LET SIT FOR TEN MINUTES
- IN A LARGE BOWL MIX ALL INGREDIENTS USING YOUR HANDS, ADD WATER AS NEEDED UNTIL DOUGH IS SOFT BUT NOT STICKY.
- KNEAD FOR 5-10 MINUTES.
- LIGHTLY FLOUR DOUGH THEN PLACE IN PLASTIC BAG.
- LET SIT IN THE FRIDGE OVERNIGHT OR FOR UP TO 3 DAYS (YOU CAN SKIP THIS.)
- TAKE OUT OF FRIDGE AND LEAVE IN A WARM PLACE TO RISE FOR A COUPLE OF HOURS.
- GREASE PIZZA PAN WITH CRISCO
- FOR FOCACCIA BAKE AT 350° OR 400°

NONNA RECOMMENDS TOPPING FOCACCIA WITH CHERRY TOMATOES, OREGANO, OLIVE OIL, GARLIC, AND CHILI FLAKES OR ANCHOVIES

THIS DOUGH RECIPE IS USED TO MAKE: FOCACIA, PIZZA, BREAD, BUNS, OR DONUTS (PG 26.)

INSALATA BACCALÀ

**SERVINGS: 10
PREP TIME: 30 MIN
BACCALÀ SOAK: 36 HOURS
COOKING TIME: 10 MIN**

HOW TO REHYDRATE BACCALÀ FOR USE, (YOU MUST DO THIS FOR ALL RECIPES.)
- WHEN YOU BUY BACCALA IT COMES DRY.
- GET THE BUTCHER TO CUT PIECES.
- TO REHYDRATE PUT IN COLD WATER FOR 36 HOURS
- CHANGE WATER EVERY DAY,
- WHEN IT'S DONE THAT'S IT YOU CAN COOK WITH IT NOW.
- YOU CAN PUT IT IN A BAG IN THE FREEZER FOR THREE OR FOUR MONTHS AFTER REHYDRATED SO IT'S READY TO USE.

INGREDIENTS
BACCALÀ (SALTED COD FISH)
CELERY
CARROT
RED PEPPER
YELLOW PEPPER
FENNEL
OLIVES
SALT
LEMON JUICE (1/2 LEMON)
A HANDFUL CLOVES GARLIC
EXTRA VIRGIN OLIVE OIL
PARSLEY FOR GARNISH ON TOP
NO SALT! SALTED COD IS ALREADY SALTY!

DIRECTIONS:
- REHYDRATE YOUR BACCALÀ
- BOIL THE BACCALÀ FOR 5-10 MIN
- STRAIN AND RINSE
- WHEN IT COOLS OFF FLAKE IT APART WITH YOUR HANDS
- ADD OTHER INGREDIENTS, TOSS GENTLY, AND SERVE WITH OTHER ANTIPASTO

DIRECTIONS

THIS RECIPE IS ALWAYS MADE ON CHRISTMAS EVE!
IT WAS NONNA ELDA'S GRANDMOTHER LAURA'S SPECIAL RECIPE.

BOIL THE REHYDRATED BACCALÀ 10 MIN THEN STRAIN GENTLY

WHEN COOL FLAKE APART WITH HANDS

CUT OFF ALL THE GREEN PIECES OF FENNEL AND CHOP INSIDE INTO BITE SIZED PIECES.

YOU CAN USE DIFFERENT VEGETABLES IF YOU LIKE, BUT TOSS VERY GENTLY OR BACCALÀ WILL BREAK.

NOTES: NONNA PUTS ENTIRE CLOVES OF GARLIC IN HERE NOT CHOPPED!

TUNA PASTA

PREP TIME: 5 MIN
COOK TIME: HALF AN HOUR

INGREDIENTS:
- COUPLE GLOVES GARLIC
- ¼ CHOPPED ONION
- 3 TBSP TOMATO PASTE
- A LITRE OF PRESERVED TOMATOES
- PESTO/ FRESH BASIL A COUPLE TBSP
- JAR OF TUNA GOOD CALLIPO BRAND
- PENNE LISCE PASTA

DIRECTIONS:
- CHOP THE TUNA UP
- FRY GARLIC AND ONIONS UNTIL IT IS A BLONDE COLOUR
- TOMATO PASTE AND JARRED TOMATOES
- BOIL 20 MIN THEN ADD CUP OF WATER
- ADD CHILI FLAKES, SALT, PEPPER
- ADD ANOTHER CUP OF WATER UNTIL IT'S A GOOD CONSISTENCY
- YOU NEED PENNE LISCE TO SERVE WITH THIS KIND (NOT PENNE RIGATE WHICH IS FOR OVEN BAKES)

ANCHOVY SPAGHETTI

SERVINGS: 4
PREP TIME: 5 MIN
COOKING TIME: 15 MIN

INGREDIENTS:
SPAGHETTI
EXTRA VIRGIN OLIVE OIL
A FEW CLOVES GARLIC
1/2 CUP OF ANCHOVIES IN OIL,
(NONNA LIKES THE PAESE MIO
BRAND OF JARRED ANCHOVIES)
A FEW TSP OF THE OIL FROM YOUR
ANCHOVY JAR
SALT
A FEW FRESH CHILI PEPPERS
HANDFUL FRESH PARSLEY CHOPPED

DIRECTIONS:
- FRY GARLIC IN EXTRA VIRGIN OLIVE OIL IN A BIG FRYING PAN WHILE SPAGHETTI IS BOILING.
- ADD THE CHILI PEPPER CHOPPED UP TO PAN.
- MIX IN THE ANCHOVIES
- ADD TWO LADLES OF THE WATER FROM YOUR BOILING PASTA.
- ADD A FEW TSP OF THE OIL FROM THE ANCHOVY JAR
- LET THE SAUCE SIMMER FOR A FEW MINUTES
- STRAIN YOUR SPAGHETTI (SHOULD BE AL DENTE) AND PUT IT DIRECTLY INTO THE FRYING PAN WITH YOUR SAUCE AND COOK IT TOGETHER FOR A COUPLE OF MINUTES

DO NOT SERVE WITH CHEESE!
SERVE WITH SOME FRESH CHOPPED PARSLEY

BACCALÀ E PATATE

SALTED COD AND POTATO STEW
SERVINGS: 5
PREP TIME: HALF HOUR
BACCALA MUST SOAK 36 HOURS BEFORE USE
COOKING TIME: 1 HOUR

DIRECTIONS

<u>INGREDIENTS</u>
5 COOKING ONIONS
1 LITRE TOMATO PUREE
1/2 OF 12OZ CAN OF PASTENE TOMATO PASTE
1/2 CUP CHOPPED CELERY
1/2 CUP CHOPPED CARROT
1/2 CUP CHOPPED PARSLEY
2 CUPS WATER
4 YELLOW POTATOES PEELED AND CUT INTO QUARTERS
A LITTLE BIT OF SALT
TSP CHILI FLAKES
5 LARGE CHUNKS OF REHYDRATED SALTED COD
SERVE WITH HARD BREAD, YOU CAN USE THE FOCACCIA (PG.6) DOUGH
RECIPE AND BAKE IT IN ONE LOAF UNTIL IT IS BROWN

<u>DIRECTIONS</u>

- REHYDRATE YOUR SALTED COD. PLACE IN COLD WATER FOR 36 HOURS, CHANGING THE WATER ONCE A DAY.
- SLICE ONIONS AND FRY UNTIL SOFT AND GOLD
- ADD TOMATO PUREE AND TOMATO PASTE
- USING PEELER, REMOVE STRINGS FROM CELERY THEN CHOP AND ADD TO SAUCE.
- ADD CARROT,
- ADD PARSLEY AND BASIL
- BRING TO BOIL
- ADD TWO CUPS WATER
- ADD POTATOES RAW
- DON'T ADD TOO MUCH SALT BECAUSE THE FISH IS SALTED
- A TSP CHILI PEPPER
- ADD FISH IN LARGE PIECES TRY NOT TO MOVE IT TOO MUCH OR YOUR FISH WILL BREAK
- COOK UNTIL YOUR POTATOES ARE SOFT
- SERVE WITH HARD ITALIAN BREAD (SEE P. 6 FOR DOUGH)

GARLIC SHRIMP

SERVINGS: 5
PREP TIME: 20 MIN
COOKING TIME: 8 MIN

DIRECTIONS

<u>INGREDIENTS</u>

PACKAGE OF SHRIMP

¾ CUP OF BUTTER MELT ON FRYING PAN

3 CLOVES CRUSHED FRESH GARLIC

1/4 CUP ITALIAN BREADCRUMBS

1 TBSP MINCED GINGER

2 TBSP ITALIAN BREADCRUMBS

HANDFUL CHOPPED PARSLEY

<u>DIRECTIONS:</u>

- CLEAN AND BUTTERFLY YOUR SHRIMP BUT LEAVE THE TAIL SHELLS ON
- LAY THE SHRIMP FLAT ON BAKING DISH
- IN A SMALL FRYING PAN MELT BUTTER, AND FRY GARLIC, GINGER, AND BREADCRUMBS
- ADD PARSLEY
- USING A SILICONE BRUSH, BRUSH YOUR BUTTER/GARLIC MIXTURE ON TOP OF YOUR SHRIMP
- BAKE AT 400 ABOUT 8 MINUTES UNTIL PINK.
- GARNISH WITH PARSLEY

NOTES: NONNA USES THIS RECIPE AND METHOD FOR COOKING OTHER TYPES OF SEAFOOD SOMETIMES, LIKE ROCK LOBSTER.

FRITTURA DI PESCE

SERVINGS: 8
PREP TIME: 30 MIN
COOKING TIME: 5 MIN PER SEAFOOD TYPE

DIRECTIONS

<u>INGREDIENTS</u>
SCALLOPS
CALAMARI
SMELT
SHRIMP
SOLE FILLET
CORNMEAL
FLOUR
COOKING OIL
FRESH PARSLEY FOR SERVING
LEMON WEDGES FOR SERVING

<u>DIRECTIONS</u>

- FILL UP A PLASTIC BAG WITH EITHER CORNMEAL OR FLOUR, AND THROW YOUR SEAFOOD IN AND TOSS IT AROUND.
- DEEP FRY IT FOR A FEW MINUTES
- YOU MUST COOK EACH TYPE OF FISH SEPARATELY TO ENSURE IT'S COOKED THE RIGHT AMOUNT OF TIME

- SCALLOPS SHOULD BE TOSED WITH FLOUR
- CALAMARI (SQUID) IS IN CORNMEAL
- SOLE FILLET IS COATED IN FLOUR
- SMELT IS CORNMEAL
- SHRIMP IS IN CORNMEAL

TIPS:THE SEAFOOD CAN'T BE TOO WET WHEN YOU TOSS IT IN THE BAG. JUST A LITTLE DAMP.

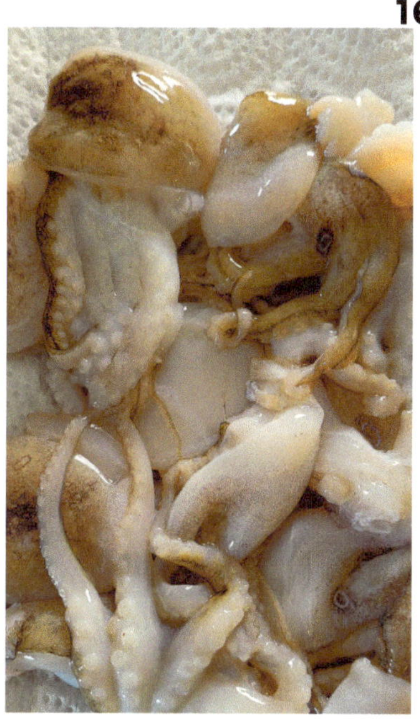

CHRISTMAS ORANGE SALAD

SERVINGS: 8
PREP TIME: 5 MIN

INGREDIENTS

RADICCHIO FENNEL

ORANGE

BLACK PEPPER, SALT

EXTRA VIRGIN OLIVE OIL

DIRECTIONS

- PREPARE AND CHOP YOUR FRESH FENNEL IN TO SLICES
- SLICE YOUR ORANGES INTO FLAT DISCS
- MIX THE TWO TOGETHER
- ADD IN YOUR RADICCHIO IN LARGE CHUNKS, USE THE LEAFY PARTS TO DECORATE
- SEASON

BROILED ASPARAGUS

SERVINGS: 5
PREP TIME: 5 MIN
COOKING TIME: 5 MIN

TIPS: DON'T PUT ASPARAGUS IN THE FRIDGE, PUT IT IN WATER LIKE FLOWERS IN A VASE AND LEAVE IT IN THE WINDOW.

INGREDIENTS

BUNCH OF ASPARAGUS
EXTRA VIRGIN OLIVE OIL
BALSAMIC VINEGAR
SALT

DIRECTIONS

- WASH YOUR ASPARAGUS,
- SNAP THE ENDS OFF WITH YOUR HANDS THEY WILL NATURALLY BREAK AT THE CORRECT SPOT.
- RUB EXTRA VIRGIN OLIVE OIL OVER THE STALKS
- ARRANGE IN ONE LAYER ON BAKING TRAY
- SEASON WITH SALT
- DRIZZLE WITH BALSAMIC VINEGAR
- BROIL, TURNING OVER ONCE
- DRIZZLE WITH MORE OLIVE OIL AND SERVE

DESSERT PLATTERS

- Dessert is served casually
- Each type of dried fruit or nut is counted up towards the 35 flavours of Christmas Eve.
- Walnuts, peanuts, and chestnuts are served
- Chestnuts are roasted before serving (in the fireplace if you have one)
- Dried fruits, raisins, and prunes are also served.
- Panettone can be sliced across instead of in tall cake sliced to create stars, these are easier to serve and eat.
- Torrone a nutty candy is often served and can be purchased at Italian grocery stores during these season.

- Fruit platters are always served after a big Italian meal but on Christmas eve we always include: pomegranates which can be broken up into handful sized pieces, pears, and clementine.
- Chiacciere (p.21)
- Crispelle (p.23)
- Pizzelle (p.25)
- We also always have Baci chocolates!

CHIACCIERE

**SERVINGS: 10
PREP TIME: HOUR
COOKING TIME: 5 MIN**

THE WORD "CHIACCIERE" MEANS CHATTER OR GOSSIP. IT IS A TRADITIONAL FESTIVAL FOOD SERVED IN MANY PARTS OF ITALY. HOWEVER, IT IS CALLED BY DIFFERENT NAMES DEPENDING ON THE LOCALE. EVERY DIFFERENT NAME REFERS TO THIS ONE DEEP FRIED CRISPY DESSERT.
IT CAN BE CALLED: CHIACCHIERE, FRAPPE, CROSTOLI, BUGIE, CENCI, MARAVIGLIAS, GALANI, OR SFRAPPOLE DEPENDING ON THE REGION.

INGREDIENTS
5 EGGS
BEAT EGGS A BIT
1 CUP SUGAR
4 TBSP WHITE WINE
3 TBSP COOKING OIL
3 TBSP ANISE EXTRACT
2 TSP BAKING POWDER
8 CUPS FLOUR
COOKING OIL
POWDERED SUGAR FOR AFTER

TOOLS
FLUTED PASTRY CUTTER
PASTA MACHINE
DEEP WOK OR PAN FOR DEEP FRYING

DIRECTIONS

- BEAT ALL THE INGREDIENTS TOGETHER EXCEPT FLOUR
- THEN ADD FLOUR
- CREATE A FIRM LOAF, AND DUST WITH FLOUR
- CUT ONE INCH SLICES AND SQUISH THEM AS SEEN BELOW
- DUST WITH FLOUR AND PASS THROUGH PASTA MACHINE
- START ON LOWER SETTING, AND WORK YOUR WAY UP MAKING THE PASTA THINNER, UNTIL IT IS AT THE TEN SETTING.
- USE FLOUR FOR DUSTING LIBERALLY

- USE FLUTED PASTRY CUTTER TO CUT STRIPS
- YOU CAN GET FANCY AND CUT A HOLE IN THE MIDDLE OF EACH STRIP AND PASS THE PASTRY THROUGH ITSELF TO CREATE A LITTLE BOW.
- DEEP FRY FOR ONE MINUTE UNTIL IT BUBBLES
- THEN DUST WITH ICING SUGAR
- THESE ARE BEST ENJOYED FRESH BUT ARE OKAY FOR A FEW DAYS

CRISPELLE

SERVINGS: 5
PREP TIME: 5 MIN
COOKING TIME: 5 MIN

IS THE MOST TRADITIONAL OF THE CHRISTMAS EVE SWEETS FOR NONNA ELDA'S FAMILY.
THIS RECIPE IS PASSED DOWN FROM NONNA'S GRANDMOTHER LAURA.

<u>INGREDIENTS</u>

400 GRAMS FLOUR

1 TSP YEAST

1 CUP WARM WATER

1 EGG

1 TSP SALT

1/2 CUP RAISINS

COOKING OIL FOR FRYING

SUGAR FOR DUSTING, REGULAR SUGAR OR POWDERED SUGAR.

OPTIONAL: THIS ISN'T TRADITIONAL BUT THEY'RE DELICIOUS WITH A LITTLE BIT OF NUTELLA ON TOP.

DIRECTIONS

<u>DIRECTIONS</u>

- PUT RAISINS IN CUP OF WARM WATER TO PLUMP BEFORE USE
- PUT YEAST IN 1 CUP WARM WATER FOR TEN MINUTES
- MIX DRY INGREDIENTS
- ADD WET INGREDIENTS
- ADD RAISINS LAST
- COVER WITH TEA TOWEL LET RISE FOR A COUPLE OF HOURS SOMEWHERE WARM
- FRY ON MEDIUM TO HIGH EAT IN ABOUT AN INCH OF COOKING OIL,
- DIP A METAL SPOON IN COLD OIL TO GREASE IT THEN SCOOP A SPOONFUL OF BATTER AND GENTLY PUT INTO FRYING PAN
- FRY UNTIL GOLDEN BROWN THEN TURN OVER
- DUST WITH EITHER REGULAR SUGAR, OR POWDERED SUGAR.

REMEMBER TO DIP YOUR SPOONS IN COLD OIL BEFORE SCOOPING THE BATTER

PIZZELLE

SERVINGS: 10
PREP TIME: 5 MIN
COOKING TIME: 1 MIN EACH

INGREDIENTS
6 EGGS
1 CUP SUGAR
3.5 CUPS FLOUR
1 CUP MELTED MARGARINE
4 TSP BAKING POWDER
2 TBSP. SAMBUCA
2 TBSP ANISE EXTRACT
YOU WILL NEED A PIZZELLE
MACHINE

DIRECTIONS
- START THE MACHINE TEN MINUTES EARLIER
- MIX ALL INGREDIENTS
- USE TWO SPOONS A BIG SPOON AND SMALL SPOON TO SCOOP YOUR BATTER OUT AND SCRAPE IT OFF THE SPOON
- COOK FOR ABOUT A MINUTE

NOTES: NONNA PREFERS A NO STICK PIZZELLE MACHINE
MUST USE MARGARINE DO NOT USE BUTTER, IT WON'T COME OUT GOOD.

DONUTS

SERVINGS: 10
PREP TIME: 3 HOURS
COOKING TIME: 5 MIN

INGREDIENTS
FOCCACCIA/PIZZA DOUGH
RECIPE FROM PAGE 6.
CHOCOLATE
SUGAR
COOKING OIL

DIRECTIONS
- MAKE YOUR DOUGH ACCORDING TO DIRECTIONS ON PAGE 6.
- MAKE SMALL BALLS THE SIZE OF THE PALM OF YOUR HAND AND DUST WITH FLOUR.
- PLACE THE BALLS ON A TRAY AND COVER WITH A TEA TOWEL FOR AN HOUR IN A WARM PLACE TO RISE
- TAKE YOUR BALLS AND PUSH A HOLE THROUGH THE MIDDLE, SHAPING A DONUT.
- COVER THE DONUTS AND LET THEM RISE AGAIN FOR ANOTHER HALF HOUR.
- DEEP FRY IN COOKING OIL UNTIL GOLDEN BROWN TURNING ONCE.
- DIP IN SUGAR
- ALTERNATIVELY, DIP IN CHOCOLATE (MELT CHOCOLATE IN A SAUCE PAN, AND ADD A SPLASH OF OIL SO THAT IT DOESN'T HARDEN COMPLETELY)
- ENJOY SAME DAY!